1 MONTH OF
FREE
READING

at

www.ForgottenBooks.com

By purchasing this book you are eligible for one month membership to ForgottenBooks.com, giving you unlimited access to our entire collection of over 1,000,000 titles via our web site and mobile apps.

To claim your free month visit:

www.forgottenbooks.com/free1249769

ISBN 978-0-428-62166-7
PIBN 11249769

erneau Masonry Legal

---IN---

OHIO.

And Elsewhere About the Globe.

and Lodges have no authority
er the "Cerneau" Rite nor any le-
right to prohibit Master Masons
m becoming members thereof.

THE CELEBRATED GOODALE LODGE INJUNCTION CASE.

DECISION IN FULL

BY ALL THE

ES OF THE CIRCUIT COURT OF FRANKLIN COUNTY, OHIO.

SUPREME COURT OF LOUISIANA

No. 19,175.

M. W. BAYLISS

versus

THE GRAND LODGE OF THE STATE OF LOUISI-
ANA.

Appeal of **M. W. Bayliss, Plaintiff,** From the Judgment
Rendered in the Civil District Court, for the Parish
of Orleans, E. K. Skinner, Judge of Division C.

SYLLABUS.

Where a masonic organization, through its regularly constituted head or agent, acting within the apparent
scope of his authority issues a large number of
printed circulars in which he mentions the head of
a rival organization by name, and calls upon his
craft not to accept the degrees "peddled by this
clandestine pretender," and urges them to "crush

this interloper in his incipiency" and when the same result in view, i. e., to prevent his craft from joining this rival body could have been obtained without using expressions which were entirely gratuitous and uncalled for, and these expressions were intended to bring said person into public contempt, ridicule or obloquy—the corporation cannot escape liability on the pleas of want of authority in the agent, justification where not proven and privilege, or that the words were not libelous.

STATEMENT OF THE CASE.

May It Please the Court:

Mr. Major W. Bayliss, a citizen of the City of Washington, D. C., sues the Grand Lodge of the State of Louisiana a masonic corporation created by an act of the Legislature of this State, for fifty thousand dollars damages for the publication of libelous edicts or circulars issued by said Grand Lodge through its Grand Master. In said edicts the plaintiff is called by name "one M. W. Bayliss, hailing from Washington D. C." and the Grand Master states that he has been advised by worthy brethren that a considerable number of Master Masons, members of lodges under our jurisdiction have received or accepted or had communicated or conferred upon them the degrees "peddled" by this clandestine pretender, appeals "to all faithful brethren to **crush this interloper** in his incipiency and declares the body **of** which Mr. Bayliss is the head, to be bogus, spurious and clandestine."

For the injury to his reputation as an honest man and to his social standing, Mr. Bayliss claims the sum of forty thousand dollars damages and for the mortification and humiliation coupled with worriment of mind over the disgrace inflicted by these libelous edicts, he claims he has suffered damages in the sum of ten thousand dollars. (Tr., pp. 40, 41, 42.)

The defendant filed an exception of vagueness, which was overruled. An exception of no cause of action was filed, coupled with an answer which "denied all and singular the allegations in plaintiff's petition contained," (Tr., p. 11), pleaded justification, (Tr., p. 17) and claimed that the circulars were privileged (Tr., p. 18). The exception of no cause of action being overruled, an amended answer was filed on March 23rd, 1909 in which were filed an exhibit (Tr., p. 23) purporting to be an extract from the report of the Grand Master to the Grand Lodge at its session of February 1st, 1909, and a report by the Committee on Masonic Law and Jurisprudence.

Plaintiff then filed a motion to show cause why the defendant should not be made to elect as to which of the pleas set forth in its answer it would adopt as its defense to plaintiff's petition, having pleaded a general denial, a justification and claimed the circulars were privileged.

The motion was overruled with written reasons for judgment. (Tr. p. 28.)

Before the opening of the case, counsel for plaintiff again moved the Court to compel the defendant to elect which defense they intended to rely upon; having pleaded a general denial, a justification and privilege. Counsel for defense thereupon admitted the issuance of the circulars, pleaded justification, admitting the truth of what plaintiff averred; but denied that Mr. Bayliss suffered any injury. The Court refused to order defendant to elect, ruling that the plea was a **general denial** and the defense was **justification.** (Tr. p 33.)

With the objections noted (Tr., pp. 59, 161) and overruled and bill of exceptions reserved, defendant's testimony was heard in an attempt to prove justification, and that plaintiff suffered no injury, in accordance with admissions of defendant's counsel and ruling of the Court.

THE EVIDENCE.

The plaintiff and appellant, M. W. Bayliss, a citizen of the City of Washington, D. C., is a Master Mason in the order of Free and Accepted Masons. He is in good standing in a Blue Lodge of said Order, which Blue Lodge is in good standing in a Grand Lodge which, in turn, is in good standing and fraternal relations with the Grand Lodge of Louisiana, appellee.

The appellant, M. W. Bayliss, is the Sovereign Commander, that is to say a chief officer, in the "Supreme Council of Sovereign Grand Inspectors General, Thirty-third and last degree of the Ancient and Accepted Scottish Rite of Freemasonry, for the United States of America, their Territories and Dependencies, Orient of New

York.'' This Rite is duly incorporated under the laws of the United States in force in the District of Columbia. The Rite he represents is not in affiliation with the ''Southern Jurisdiction Rite,'' nor with the ''Northern Jurisdiction Rite'' of Scottish Rite Masonry, nor with the Grand Lodge of Louisiana, a corporation of this State, created by Act of the Legislature of 1816. The Grand Lodge of Louisiana recognizes the masonic legitimacy of the Northern Jurisdiction Rite, and also of the Southern Jurisdiction Rite with which its members affiliate.

In January or early part of February, 1908, Mr. Henderson, one of the subordinate officers of the Rite of which Mr. Bayliss is the head, visited New Orleans with the view of planting their Rite among the Master Masons of Louisiana, none but Master Masons being eligible to membership, and he initiated a dozen or more with the view of organizing a ''consistory'' a subordinate lodge of his Rite. Some question arose as to whether Master Masons in Louisiana could consistently join this particular Rite, and the plaintiff sought and obtained a conference with Mr. J. C. Drew, the Grand Master of the Grand Lodge of Louisiana, on this subject, and the Grand Master promised him that he would give him a hearing before a committee or before the Grand Lodge, (Tr., p. 163) and the plaintiff left with that understanding (which is not denied) for his home in Washington.

It appears by the record that some correspondence was had between Germania Masonic Lodge No. 46, in this City and the Grand Master, and the edicts which form the basis of this suit were issued and published by the Grand Master. Mr. Bayliss, instead of getting information as to his hearing on the merits of his Rite received these publications and he wrote **Pamphlet** D 2 in explanation of the circumstances and complained of the Grand Master's failure to keep his promise.

The edicts on which this suit is based are in evidence, proved and admitted, (Tr., p. 23) to have been issued by the Grand Master, countersigned and sealed by the Grand Secretary of the corporation in their official capacity, and within the scope of their authority. (Tr., p. 198.)

The bill for the printing of one thousand of these circulars is in evidence and proved to have been **paid by** the **corporation.**. The original edict was sent to the printer. (Tr., pp. 187-8.) The edicts were republished in several masonic magazines throughout the **U**nited States.

The defendant relies on the offer of ex parte reports from Grand Lodges of various States to prove that the words complained of are common expressions understood by all Masons, but more particularly and purposely (and in spite of the ruling of the trial Judge and admission of counsel for defendant Tr., pp. 121 and 122) to show that the Rite represented by Mr. Bayliss was not recognized by the Grand Lodge of those several States. And this had its effect on the mind of the Judge a quo.

The defendant also offered in evidence a pamphlet (D 2) published by Mr. Bayliss, an answer to the edicts of the Grand Master, for the purpose of showing that Mr. Bayliss had retaliated in kind. It is to be noted here that the defendant has not pleaded nor made this an issue in the case. It was an afterthought. (See objection to testimony, Tr., p. 71.)

THE OPINION OF THE LOWER COURT.

The distiguished trial Judge dismissed the suit upon three grounds only, to-wit: 1. That the plaintiff was at fault himself in the initiation of the controversy, 2. that he was again at fault in retaliation, and 3. that he does not find the language libelous or malicious. The judgment must stand or fall here upon one or all of these propositions.

I.

We respectfully submit, 1. That the facts stated in the opinion do not support a charge of moral or legal fault in either proposition. 2. That the facts recited in the opinion and constituting the basis of finding decisive substantial legal fault in the plaintiff, in either event do not measure up to that high degree of fault, contributory or retaliative, which in law relieves the plaintiff of his otherwise confessed case. It should have been such fault as would be actionable independently of the fault originally complained of. And furthermore it should have been specially pleaded and an issue in the case. It was never pleaded.

II.

On the proposition that the plaintiff was in fatal fault at the inception of this controversy, the learned trial Judge culled from the entire record, as it was proper for him to do, the greatest alleged fault made by the plaintiff in this:

> "Mr. Bayliss (D. 2, p. 19) says: 'During our interview the Grand Master asked us if we had organized. We answered that we had not.' This is the only question he asked relative to our Rite, and we replied without the least equivocation or mental reservation. We took it for granted that he knew degrees had been given, and that he desired to know whether or not bodies had been organized. If he desired to learn whether or not degrees had been given he should have asked the question. We would have furnished any information he wished."

It is submitted in frankness and confidence that, nothing found in the matter above quoted from the opinion can be construed as evasive or showing purpose to conceal any important information. The answer to the question as to "whether we had organized?" was direct, its own self explanation and full exculpation from such fault as to deny relief to the plaintiff. The plaintiff answered truthfully the question propounded to him, and gave a reason sustained by the record for not making the further answer now complained of. He is sustained for a belief that the Grand Master knew then of initiations. It will not be forgotten that this conference between these high brother masons was upon the subject of **organizing a consistory,** (Pamphlet D. 1., Tr. p. 160) and the Grand Master knew it, (Pamphlet D 3, p.

22); and for an opportunity to plaintiff to show the masonic merits of his Rite. (Tr., pp. 114, 125.) We further submit that the transcript not only upholds the statement of the plaintiff that he supposed that the Grand Master knew of the initiations, that in truth and in fact he did know it, but also, that the plaintiff left that conference believing he had the right not only of initiation but of organization, and was not otherwise apprised until the publication of the libels complained of came to his hands in Washington shortly after their appearance through the mails.

III.

It cannot escape the attention of this Court that the opinion of the learned trial Judge leading down to his finding of defensive initiative fault on the part of the plaintiff, confesses, **ex necessitate** finding first, actionable fault of the Grand Master in such manner as to bind the Grand Lodge, or the body corporate, also leads down to the second proposition of retaliative fault on plaintiff's part by a like confession of first finding legally actionable fault in the publications of the slanderous edicts. We submit that it does not answer the demand of the law which "obliges him by whose fault it happened to repair it," to say "these edicts were evidently intended to be confidential to the Masonic Order, but evidently became public, and are the basis of this suit." The intention is shown by the results and effects.

Now, then, we submit that, after traveling through the record to follow the trend of the conclusions reached by the trial Judge who found original and continuing actionable fault excused by lack of an answer "not entirely frank and complete," although not deceptive or misleading and in a natural complaint of a malicious publication spread abroad whether so intended to be or not, "that the Grand Master violated a promise to allow a hearing regarding the merits of the Scottish Rite represented by him." Plaintiff went to the Grand Master for a conference, got the promise of a hearing on the merits of his Rite, left believing that he would get it, but instead was personally branded in most burning and scandalous language. Yet, because a gentleman complains under such galling wounds of a broken promise, has he lost his case?

We respectfully challenge a comparison of the facts in this case with those cited in the opinion, or that may be in the brief of opposing counsel, to show the utter want of fatal initiative or retaliative fault of the plaintiff. The proposition that the defendant has justified its calumnies on these grounds fails. And. losing this defense, the case is closed against it. We again claim that the defense should have been specially pleaded. (See authorities quoted hereafter.)

IV.

Finally on these propositions. We have above contended that the conclusion reached by the learned trial Judge as to conditions created by the plaintiff is not supported by the record. We submit that in further leading to his judgment of the case he was in greater error in concluding that "these edicts of the Grand Master were invited by this surreptitious invasion of the jurisdiction of the Grand Lodge of Louisiana over the partially successful attempt to swerve their allegiance to it, members of recognized masonic bodies in this State." This sentence doubtless forced from the bench by the nature of the case as he saw it, from the great array of Grand Lodge reports admitted only to prove that the words used were common expressions, manifests the wisdom of that law which holds that the failed pleadings in a case like this, is a continuing aggravation of the libel and consequent damages.

We will be excused for expressing the apprehension that the enthusiasm of the eminent counsel for defendant of which he was once the head and one of its honored members led off the trial Judge from the threshold of the opinion to its conclusions, into strange fields of learning.

V.

The good faith and proof of no initiative fault on the part of plaintiff is borne out by the record. (See Tr., pp. 49, 50, 67, 114, 124, 125, 127, and defendant's own witness, Tr., pp. 213, 215.)

The trial Judge says in his decison:

"Mr. Bayliss in his pamphlet 'D 2' complains that the Grand Master violated a promise to allow a hearing regarding the merits of the Scottish Rite represented by him. Admitting this, **Mr. Bayliss** concedes that he knew there was objection to the admission of his Rite, which he was endeavoring to overcome, and in the meantime was either himself or by deputy initiating regular Masons into his unrecognized and hence masonically illegal body.''

We respectfully submit that neither by the record nor by any process of deduction does Mr. Bayliss make such concession. He heard no objection, knew of no masonic law in this jurisdiction prohibiting the conferring of his degrees and believed there was none, which belief is corroborated by defendant's own witness F. W. Heroy (Tr. pp. 213, 215), and neither were degrees conferred in the meantime. (Tr., p. 127.) Knowing what had been done in Arkansas, and rescinded upon proper explanation he sought an interview with the Grand Master, believing that a due regard to his masonic obligations irrespective of his sense of justice, would insure him a hearing and prevent possible adverse action. This is plainly set forth in the following quotation from near the bottom of page 18 of pamphlet ''D-2.''

''While in Little Rock we learned that the Grand Master of La., might be induced by our opponents to interfere with our work in that State. Upon completion of our business in Arkansas, we went to New Orleans for the purpose of interviewing the Grand Master, if possible, and ascertaining whether or not we would be heard before being condemned.''

VI.

"I do not find the language libelous or malicious."

With these words the Judge a quo dismisses the question of libel vel non.

We respectfully submit that his opinion is not in harmony with the settled jurisprudence and findings of the Courts of this State and country.

It is not what the Grand Master had in mind or what the well posted Mason may understand by the words '"clandestine pretender" and "interloper" or a peddler of masonic degrees, but what the ordinary mind, or any one reading those words will understand.

Taking the specific words complained of in their common acceptation and meaning ,as plain people and the plain law does, rather than in their lodge room parlance, the standard dictionary gives the following definitions: "Clandestine," kept secret for a purpose; concealed; surreptitious; underhand. "Pretender," one who makes false or exaggerated profession or display; hypocrite; dissembler. "Interloper," one who intrudes into a profession, office, etc., belonging to another; one who thrusts himself into a place without right. "Peddler," one who sells in small quantities out of a stock carried from house to house; to hawk; to dispense little by little. "Spurious," not from the proper sources or from a pretended source; not genuine; false; forged; conterfeit; illegitimate. These are samples of the epithets contained in the publications, and "sharper than a serpent's tooth" they sting the personal character and reputation of the plaintiff, and they are filled with venom.

What better proof of what the ordinary mind, **even that of a mason,** will understand by these words, than the testimony of defendant's own witness.

Mr. Josiah Gross, witness for **defendant** in his testimony on page 171 of the transcript, says:

> Q. Can you tell what the Masonic understanding is of one who is a peddler by (sic) being a clandestine pretender?
> A. **He is a FRAUD.**

In the digest of American cases cited **in Newell on Slander and Libel, (2nd. Ed.), p. 50, par. 34,** it has been held libelous to publish of a man **in writing or print** "he is a hog," to call an attorney "a shyster," to call a man a "skunk." To charge a person with being "a drunkard," "a cuckold" a "tory." To designate an editor of a neighboring newspaper "an ill-natured manikin 'a' mouse most magnanimous," "a vermin small."

And on page 58, digest of English cases, par. 1, it is libelous to **write** and **publish** of a man that he is "an infernal villain" an "impostor" hypocrite," a "frozen snake."

In paragraph 3, ironical praise may be a libel, calling an attorney "an honest lawyer." To impute to a Presbyterian "gross intolerance" in not allowing his hearse to be used at the funeral of his Roman Catholic servant. Page 60, paragraph 10, it is libelous to call a man a "black-leg" or a "black-sheep."

Illustrations (page 78). To state **in writing** that a man has turned into an enormous swine and lives on lame horses'' and ''will remain a swine the rest of his days'' is libelous.

> ''Scandalous matter is not necessary to make a libel. It is enough if the defendant induce an ill opinion to be had of the plaintiff or make him ridiculons or comptemptible.
>
> ''To **say** of a man he is a dishonest man is **not** actionable, but to **publish** so or to put it upon **posts is** actionable. Skinner 124.''

We believe that the trial Judge's third and last reason for dismissing plaintiff's suit is not well founded and not borne out by the evidence nor in harmony with the jurisprudence of the land.

ARGUMENT.

I.

This is a libel suit and not a suit to determine the relative merits of the two rival Rites advocated by the parties to this suit. And under the ruling of the trial Judge, sustaining plaintiff's objection, all evidence which may tend to prove the relative merits of the two Rites is to be disregarded. And whether the Rite of which Mr. Bayliss is the head be recognized or not by the defendant, cannot be considered by your Honors, in determining whether Mr. Bayliss has made out a case of libel against the Grand Lodge of Louisiana, for calling him by name an **interloper**, a **clandestine pretender** and a **peddler** of **bogus, spurious** and **clandestine Masonic** degrees.

Letter of Secretary Josiah Gross, February, 1908.

In the letter of the secretary of Germania Lodge No. 46, in the City of New Orleans, addressed to Grand Master J. C. **Drew** on the 27th day of February, 1908, the secretary, Mr. Josiah Gross, stated that he had been invited to join in the **formation of a consistory** of plaintiff's Scottish Rite.

This letter anticipated both the lack of information on the part of the Grand Master, and respectfully suggested to him a means of being fully informed by a conference with plaintiff. It reads as follows:

> "If as may be probable, you are not yet fully informed as to the claims of the jurisdiction of the United States, would you have any objection to a conference with the brethren now engaged in establishing this consistory, for the benefit of all concerned."

The silence is ominous on this point in the Grand Master's answer to this letter, as it is upon the information by telegram that the "Grand Lodge of Arkansas had decided favorably to the Bayliss committee."

And, another significant fact in this letter is the necessity for immediate action to save jeopardizing "the standing of many well-meaning brethren, who now believe that they are within their rights in assisting the new organization."

So it is, it is respectfully insisted, that this initial step begins the disclosure of a reckless and depraved disregard for the rights of the plaintiff, because the Grand Master had full information that should have led him to an amicable adjustment of the annoyance and saved the humiliation that must follow alike to the plaintiff and the Grand Lodge of Louisiana. The record of the testimony shows a conference which plaintiff left, believing he would meet no opposition. In view of the expressed belief of Mr. Gross and the other well-meaning Master Masons, in their right to join plaintiff's consistory, it was gross carelessness and inexcusable negligence, if not positive design to harm the plaintiff, in not making a reasonable investigation and granting Bayliss a hearing as promised in the interview.

The testimony teems with instances to show that Mr. Bayliss acted in good faith throughout. For instance at page 49 of the transcript, in cross-examination by Mr. Buck:

> Q. Did you not know before you came here that the Grand Lodge of Louisiana had acted upon this question as to what Scottish Rite bodies it would recognize in this State?

A. No, sir; I did not know it, and I made efforts to find out from one who, I was told, was District Deputy Grand Master of your Lodge, and I was told by him that there was no law on your record which prevented members from joining if they saw fit. * * *

Q. You knew if you got into a jurisdiction holding the view that the Grand Lodge of Louisiana was holding, that you would cause trouble? You know that?

A. No, sir; I do not.

Q. You certainly ought to have known it as a Mason.

A. Brother Buck, how could you expect me to know when the members of your own Grand Lodge didn't know, a gentleman took the Code down and examined it to answer my question.

And see, Tr., p. 67.

And again at page 114:

By Mr. McClurg:

"You have stated that you came here by invitation from Master Masons of Louisiana?

A. A letter written to me, individually, by Masons, owing allegiance to the Grand Lodge of Louisiana, relative to the organization of Scottish Rite Bodies in the State of Louisiana.

And see, Tr., p. 124.

At transcript page 125, we find the following:

Q. What was his name?

A. Mr. Drew, I am not sure about the initials; I showed him my certificate as a Mason, my patents, my receipts and convinced him that I was alright, and I told him what had been done in Arkansas, and showed him a copy of the report of the committee, as unanimously adopted there and asked him if he would give us a hearing before he took any action. He promised me he would—that was my understanding and I left him, believing that before anything was done here I would be called upon to appear before a committee or before the Grand Lodge, or in some way to explain this matter; and shortly after I got home the edicts were issued.

And again at page 127 of the transcript:

By Mr. Bayliss:

A. So far as my knowledge goes, I never did a thing to offend the Grand Lodge of Louisiana, or any member, my aim was to do what was right, and every move I have made was to gain honest information so as to avoid over-stepping any law and just as soon as the Grand Master issued his edicts all work was stopped here, and I inquired where he got his authority, whether there was any such law here. I have a copy of the Constitution, and I can find no such law in it and I know of no law to-day, only by hearsay, that there is anything against it. I know of nothing by official printed information that the Grand Lodge has passed any law or amended its Constitution in any way to affect the Scottish Rite Masonry.

And defendant's own witness, Fred W. Heroy, in his examination by Mr. Buck, testifies:

Q. Did you and he discuss the matter of the law of the Grand Lodge of Louisiana on the subject of Scottish Rite Masonry.?

A.   Who do you mean by "he?"

Q.   Mr. Henderson and you?

A.   Yes, Mr. Henderson.

Q.   What action did you reach?

A.   I reached the conclusion that there was no law that would interfere in my receiving the Scottish Rite degrees.

Q.   How did you reach that conclusion?

A.   After asking question of those I thought ought to know.

Q.   Whom did you ask?

A.   I asked a large number of people in this city here.

Q.   Name some of them, please?

A.   To come right down to it specifically and finally, among others, one day I came into the Fire Prevention Bureau building and was talking to a Mr. Rickey, there were others there also, but I talked to him.

And on page 215, of the transcript, same witness:

A.   Mr. Rickey told me he was going to refer the matter to you (meaning Mr. Buck), and I said: "Please let me know what Brother Buck thinks about it." He said: "I think he will say that it is clandestine." I said: "Let me know. The next day I saw him and he told me that you (Mr. Buck) knew of nothing that would prevent him from joining the aforesaid Scottish Rite (Bayliss') but you (Mr. Buck), advised him, Brother Rickey, to join the Scottish Rite that was down here in the city."

It is both significant and amusing to notice how the name of "Bayliss" was bandied in the letters and edicts and how it was avoided to be written at all in the report to the Grand Lodge. Like the chiseling a name off the arch of Cabin John's bridge; made it more prominent.

II.

GRAND MASTER DREW'S EDICT. MARCH 14TH, 1908.

It begins: "A communication has been addressed to me, in my official capacity as Grand Master," and ends, "J. C. Drew, Grand Master." Ridicule and contempt is evidenced in its first lines: "by one M. W. Bayliss, hailing from Washington, D. C." Then follows the false and terribly reacting declaration that, "after very careful consideration and the most exhaustive research into this matter." And the next part of the sentence: "I have arrived at a positive and definite conclusion," carries in it one of the most significant elements of legal malicious purpose in the whole case; in that, he expresses a positive conviction of an erroneous and to the defendant, a most unfortunate conclusion; thereby, as it will be pointed out later on, eliminating consideration by the Court of citations to information and forcing his official deductions to stand along in justification of what he writes and publishes.

It is respectfully submitted, that a false statement heretofore pointed out, in skilfully and for a deliberately deceptive purpose added, when the Grand Master, undertaking to elude and "brace up," writes his brethren, "I find, after the most careful examination and probing this matter to the bottom, that the said Mr. Major W. Bayliss is the presiding officer of the Supreme Council of Sovereign Grand Inspectors General, etc, A. & A. S. R., and that said Body is designated by some as the Bayliss-Gibson Body, (specifically denied in the proof) which is known to be a branch of the "**Cerneau**" Body of Masonry which has been declared clandestine by the Grand Lodges of Ohio, Iowa, Massachusetts, Pennsylvania and many others." Strangely enough, he failed to state his information of the action of the Grand Lodge of Arkansas. (See letter of Gross, D. 1.)

Such conduct, we submit, in connection with the purpose to protect the membership and source of revenue of the Southern Scottish Rite Masonry, distinctly shows the envious malice of the Grand Master—the vicious intention to drive out the Supreme Council of the plaintiff even though the destruction of the plaintiff himself became, as he in fact deemed it, a necessity to that end, and "crush this interloper in his incipiency."

Jurisdictional Power, Authority, Agency, "Now therefore, brethren, upon me, as your chosen Grand Master, is imposed the duty of seeing the laws and regulations of this Grand Lodge are duly and strictly enforced, and from this sworn duty I shall not swerve or turn aside." And then what? "The fact having been clearly established to my mind beyond any reasonable doubt whatever, that the Cerneau Bodies are clandestine, I therefore, by virtue of authority vested in me as Grand

Master of the most worshipful Grand Lodge of the State of Louisiana F. and A. M. do hereby declare the Bodies calling themselves the Supreme Council of the Sovereign Inspectors General of the Thirtythird and last degree, Ancient and Accepted Scottish Rite for the United States of America, their Territorities and Dependences, and commonly known as the Cernean Rite, to be bogus, spurious, and clandestine, and that they ought not to be countenanced or recognized in any manner by brethren under obedience to this Grand Lodge." He proceeds then to warn the membership under penalty of expulsion, not to join it, and to command, "the Grand Secretary shall furnish every lodge in his Grand Jurisdiction with a copy of this communication, and the same be read in open lodge, so all the Brethren be informed." (Black-letters ours.)

III.

GRAND MASTER DREW'S EDICT OF MARCH 24TH, 1908.

Recalling with approval his previous edict, more directly aimed at the Rite, his first paragraph in his edict of March 24th, begins also in ridicule and contempt, plainly manifest, for "one M. W. Bayliss, claiming to be the head" etc., "who had communicated or conferred upon them the degrees 'peddled' by this clandestine pretender." Your Honors have said, as we will point out, that this "thrust was not only gratuitous but libelous." **Under**-standing the task he was to perform in the work of rivalry among honorable free Masons he paved the way to his point by excusing the ignorance of those who believed, (and we are informed by the letter of Mr. Josiah Gross, that there were "many well-meaning men" who entertained the belief), "that the Grand Lodge has control only of the Three Symbolic **D**egrees; that it takes no cognizance of the other degrees or branches of Masonry." He then plans a way by which these Master Masons may escape masonic death by confession and recantation which he required the Masters of the **L**odges to exact and to "heal" the offending members in the manner and upon the conditions named by him. Here the shaft is driven its full length into the plaintiff. No necessity of "further argument **or proof as to the spurious and clandestine character of 'Bayliss' masonry, nor of my duty and authority to interfere in the premises.** Louisiana masonry has fought this battle many years ago, as other States have done, where the clandestines, encouraged by temporary success, crowned their unlawful encroachments by selling even the three fundamental degrees. I appeal to all faithful brethren **to crush this interloper** in his incipiency and keep the fire-brands of discord and confusion out of **our Temple.**" Signed J. C. **D**rew, Grand Master, and attested under seal of the Grand Lodge by Richard Lambert, Grand Secretary. (Our black-letters.) **T**his edict is dismissed for the present with the utmost confidence that the Court appreciates its animus toward plaintiff and will give it due consideration in adjudging the justice and legality of the plaintiff's claim.

IV.

GRAND MASTER DREW'S THIRD LETTER, APRIL 23RD, 1908.

(Pamphlet D-3, page 25.)

"As the attitude of the Grand Lodge towards the so-called Cerneau Rite does not seem to be generally known to the Craft" etc. "The different circulars (the edicts) have been adversely criticised and doubt as to the correctness as to the Grand Master's position publicly express-ed," is the language used in the opening of this communication. Then follows the beginning of the shameless dodge followed up to the moment. "Many probably accepting that publication ('Square and Compass') as **quasi** official, while it utterances must be accepted as wholly unofficial and personal." The Court will readily understand the change that came over the spirit of his dreams. "I submit further proof that it is not only my right, but my bounden duty to take drastic measures, if necessary, **to crush this interloper in his incipiency.**" It seems, verily, that his own craft evinced a spirit of rebellion against his high-handed purpose to use their lodges to crush this interloper, or to meddle with Scottish Rites.

The effort to take shelter behind Mr. Buck serves him no good purpose. It is but the agonizing shriek of a guilty conscience. The report, in the legal and logical view of the instant case, has not been, nor can it be justified in law; its republication here for an express purpose fails. The comparison is deadening. The sensible temper of that report condemns the ill-temper here.

The post-script paragraph intentionally, it is believed, omitted to cite any reference to plaintiff's Lodge and Grand Lodge in which he was in good standing, and with which the Grand Lodge of Louisiana was in fraternal communication as it did to the action taken by the Arkansas Masons. He did not know, as he might have known, and should have known, as it was his duty to know, that plaintiff's Rite was endorsed by a public, recorded act of incorporation under the laws of the United States in force in the District of Columbia. The Grand Master was so strenuously taken to task by Louisiana Masons that he was compelled to initiate his defense against his own Kith and Kin.

V.

REPORT TO GRAND LODGE, FEBRUARY, 1909.

In the opening breath of acting Grand Master Null's report of the matter here under investigation to his Grand Lodge, he expresses satisfaction in suppressing "the attempted introduction of Cernauism into this State." So completely had Grand Master Drew dealt the blow and with such "little difficulty or friction," he proceeded to declare, "it is safe to say that the peace and harmony of our different subordinate bodies will never again be threatened by its re-appearance." Then he boasts of the pleasure it gave him in "making a part of this report as an appendix, the circular letters and papers in connection," and to express the "hope that you will give them due consideration and weight and approve the acts of your official head." Hence, it is, by the first official mention by the "official head," to the Grand Lodge, the libel of nearly a year's standing was approved, reiterated, republished and intensely aggravated.

The reassertion and the republication given in the first paragraph of the report is made all the more personally offensive and publicly harmful to the plaintiff, because acting Grand Master Null made them after knowledge of the fact, "that the person—a Master Mason—I am informed, in good standing in a lodge under the jurisdiction of a Grand Lodge with which this Grand Lodge is in fraternal communication, whose name appears in these circulars, has taken personal exception to them on the ground that they contain references to him as a man which he considered libelous and defamatory." Plaintiff had complained to the Court to redress the wrong perpetrated against him by the "fault" of the Grand Master; who with the knowledge of plaintiff's masonic good standing, not only refused to make an effort to "repair it," but proceeds to ridicule the effort of plaintiff to seek compensation, in a measure, for the injury, in the Courts of this State, "in the modest sum of fifty thousand dollars," and he endorses the advice that the suit "need not be taken seriously."

However, his evident guilty conscience forced his pen at once into a further defensive line, and into wholly erroneous statements wherein he advises the Grand Lodge that "the acts of the Grand Master are not the acts of the Grand Lodge until in terms approved by it;" and in that, "the Grand Lodge is not concerned with the particular verbiage or expression which the Grand Master employed in his communication to the Masons of this jurisdiction." The law, we submit, is exactly the reverse. The unquestioned proof made by defendant's own witnesses is that in vacation the Grand Master is the Grand Lodge and, right or wrong, must be, and in fact was literally obeyed. (Trans., p. 198.) The apologetic explanations in the next paragraphs not only show an effort to induce a false construction of his "particular verbiage" by the Craft, but it is equivalent to a confession of his wrong, and is in fact a further publication thereof.

Nothing can be more convincingly apparent, it is respectfully submitted, than the false and deceptive appeals of the Grand Master for a different construction by the Grand Lodge of his "particular verbiage" than that the spirit in which it was written or that which, in common interpretation, it imparts and means. What "mailed hand" wrote this? The "**conclusion**" of the "official head" that the "Grand Lodge should limit itself" in considering the action of the Grand Master, "to the expression of approval or disapproval to this scope and intent, without reference to any foreign or personal comment not a part of the law of this grand jurisdiction on the subject," is not well taken, it is not sound.

One truth is found in the report: "Obviously, it was therefore, not only the Grand Master's right, but his duty, to warn the Craft under his jurisdiction." But the correlative truth, that it was his duty to warn within reasonable bounds and **in language free from malicious libel,** especially personal defamation to that "person, a Master Mason, whose name appears in these circulars—actually ashamed or afraid to write it, hence that **name** does not appear in the report—eo **no**mine, but it is read between the lines.

Finally: the report affirms the despotic power of the Grand Master, **ad interim,** in that it points out that "after the publication of the circulars" twelve Master Masons in the City of New Orleans, did what? "Admitted, in response to the edict, in that regard, that they had had masonic communication with **the party.** The extent of it was not ascertained; but, in open lodge, the brethren declared their withdrawal and recantation."

"The party?" **P**en paralysis prevented his writing "M. W. Bayliss."

A smitten conscience and the fear of the law forbade him to name the plaintiff in his report to the Grand **L**odge. In fear, ridicule and contempt, he refers to plaintiff as "the person," "the party," etc. Surely a legal truth had been whispered into his ear. He undertook in that report to cajole the Grand Lodge to adopt a false construction and meaning of what he had published. The report is false; so palpably false in fact and in law, that it reads itself beyond the reach of privilege, mitigation or justification.

The studied deliberation with which the defamatory language of the official edicts were thought out, written out, printed, mailed and published to the hundreds of subordinate lodges to be read to and by the thirteen thousand Masons in Louisiana, the hundreds of thousand of Masons in the United States and throughout the masonic world, and by others in whose hands these edicts fell; is so positively and unequivocally expressive of ill-will toward the plaintiff personally and of purpose direct to bring him into contempt, ridicule and hatred and to injure him, that it is absolutely indefensible by justification or by any other means known to the law.

Indeed, to the plaintiff, or to any decent man, with wife, and his children to follow him, with friends and associates to remember him, with a character and reputation of half a century's making, and, of which he may well be proud, these edicts appear as "cruel as death, as hungry as the grave."

It should have been enough, entirely enough, for this assault to have stopped with an exposure of the masonic unsoundness of the Scottish Rite which the plaintiff sought to plant here in masonic method and without violation of law. It is respectfully submitted, it is impossible to follow the assault in its ill temper beyond the condemnation of the Rite itself into a mercilessly savage attack upon the personal character and reputation of the man, without discovering moral, legal vemon, malice in law and malice in fact. As was said by the Louisiana Supreme Court in the **Lescale vs. Schwartz case:** "There was no necessity for the defendants to refer to the plaintiff. It was wholly gratuitous. They went out of their way to assail him in the manner complained of" "a mere cover from under which to perpetrate an unwarrantable and uncalled for assault."

VI.

So then, we have a case where the Grand Lodge put one at its head and clothed him with every power it possessed, to be exercised at his discretion in vacation for and on its behalf. That by and through this authorized agent, acting within the scope of his duties and authority, we find that Grand Lodge itself bursting forth in two distinct scurrilously defamatory edicts ten days apart, in most premediated deliberation, against the Scottish Rite under the Supreme Council of the United States, etc., and also against the plaintiff, a Master Mason in good standing in a Lodge of good standing, and in masonic correspondence and fraternity with itself. Admitting, for the sake of argument, the right to supervise such branches, be granted, there could be no license to slander either the Rite itself or any of its officers. In vacation the Grand Master was the Grand Lodge, and as held by the lower Court in passing upon the exceptions to the petition, the Grand Lodge was and is responsible for his official acts.

In the present light of this developed case, it seems to be beyond doubt that the controlling motive for the publication complained of rested in the rivalry which the Supreme Council Scottish Rite proposed to institute in the

State of Louisiana with the Southern Jurisdiction Scottish Rite already firmly established here, and that the Grand Lodge espoused the cause of the Southern Jurisdiction and, deliberately, with malice in law, undertook to strike the Rite represented by Mr. Bayliss and its chief officer personally a crushing blow.

VII.

PRIOR PUBLICATIONS—GRAND LODGE REPORTS.

to the effect that "reports and rumors previously existing" is no justification for publishing defamatory matter.

In Billet vs. Times-Democrat Pub. Co., 107 La. 759, Judge Monroe quoted in the opinion:

> "In giving currency to libelous and slanderous reports and publications, a party is as much responsible, civilly and criminally, as if he had originated the defamation. Tale bearers are as bad as tale makers. To justify by proving the truth of the facts stated, the defendant not only assumed the burden of proving the statements, but of proving that those statements were true."

This, we submit, disposes of the adverse action by other Lodges and the plea and the proof fall:

It will certainly not be claimed by defendant's counsel that a single slanderous word, sentence or line in either edict was proven to be true. Then the plea of justification having failed in the proof, the plea itself serves, says the law, "as an aggravating circumstance" to be taken into consideration in estimating the damages. The motive with which the plea was made necessarily follows the motive that prompted the publications.

> "Neither reasonable cause to believe a libelous charge is a defense for its publication. (Burt's case, Mass. 13 L. R. A. 97) nor the mere belief in the truth of the publication is necessarily enough

to constitute 'good faith' on the part of the publisher; there must have been an absence of negligence as well as improper motives in making the publication. It must have been honestly made in the belief of its truth and upon reasonable grounds for its belief, after the exercise of such means to verify its truth as would be taken by a man of ordinary prudence.''

VIII.

THE PLEAS, OR ANSWERS. "EXHIBITS 'A' AND 'B.' "

No retraction or disavowal is shown. At the utmost an explanation, or excuse, after suit brought is reported to the Grand Lodge about ten months later and its action is equivalent to a direct approval of what had been done by the Grand Master. The report in itself an insulting aggravation of long standing wrong, was adopted even though done in a shielding and apologetic way. To turn back now and recall all of the official masonic and Court documents in their chronological order and give all the usual interpretation, we submit that each of them but intensify the original injury.

"A subsequent article not containing a disa_vowal or retraction but attempting to put a new construction upon the libel is not admissible as a mitigating circumstance.'' **25 Cyc. L. &. Pra. 424.**

Of course the Court will remember that no effort was made, as it could not be, to show that either the Grand Master or the Grand Lodge undertook to correct the wrong by sending out a letter or edict to the Lodges explaining, retracting or disavowing a purpose to wrong. In short, the original libel was not only permitted to stand for all the injury it was worth, but has been exaggerated in every kind of publication thereof since, and will be until the case is finally closed.

"The Court found that the publication of the libel was followed, upon the next day, by a recantation, and that the reputation of the plaintiff was vindicated by an article written by the **employee** by whom the libel had been penned and subsequently published in the same paper. Nevertheless, it was said, 'The injury has been done—**vox semel missa non revertit.** The slander circulated by one issue of the paper could not be wholly obliterated by recantation in another.' As if quoting from the instant case, Judge Monroe, in **Billet's case,** proceeded to note, **'In the case at bar there has been no** recantation, nor reparation of any kind. On the contrary, the defendant has affirmed the truth of the libel complained of by averments in its pleadings which it has failed to sustain by proof.' The judgment appealed from was annulled and judgment entered for plaintiff.'' (See also **New Orleans Times case, 25 La. Ann. 170.**)

In **Covington vs. Robertson, 111 La. 342**, this Court approves the rules laid down in **Am. & Eng. Encyc. of Law**, pp. 998 and 1029, that:

> "When the publications of libelous or slanderous matter is shielded by no privilege, it will be no defense, either in a civil or criminal proceeding, that the defendant in good faith believed the charge to be true, and otherwise acted without malice, and that the fact that the defendant had probable cause for such belief does not alter the rule."

It will be noted by the Court that the edicts do not disclose upon what information or authority they were published. We are left to infer from the course of the defendant's counsel on the trial that the basis for the publications rested upon the **ex part**e declarations of other lodges.

And, further, in the **Covington** case:

> "Assuming that defendant was honestly convinced that plaintiff was guilty of the crime with which he charged him, he reached his conclusions upon statements made to him by Zachary, which carried no probative force to any reasonably prudent man and the circumstances of which he himself had personal knowledge, were totally insufficient to have justified him in making the charge he did."

The parallel is plain.

AUTHORITIES IN SUPPORT OF PLAINTIFF'S ARGUMENT.

This is an action for **libel**, based on the publications issued by the Grand Master of the Grand Lodge of the State of **Louisiana**.

An action for libel in Louisiana is based on the statutory provisions of the Civil Code (Article 2315), which declares that "every act **whatever** of man which causes damage to another obliges him by whose fault it happened to repair it."

I.

LIBEL.

"The term 'libel' includes 'every written **publication** which implies or may be generally understood to imply **reproach** ,dishonor, **scandal or ridicule** to any person. Such **written** publication, though not charging a punishable offense, is nevertheless libelous if it **tends** to subject the party to whom it refers to social disgrace, **public distrust**, hatred, ridicule, **or contempt.**"
.**Words and Phrases, Vol. 5. verbo Libel, p. 4117. Long** line of authorities.

"A libel is a publication, whether in writing, printing, **picture**, effigy, or other fixed **representation** to the eye, which exposes any person to

hatred, ridicule, or obloquy, or which causes him to
be shunned, or which has a tendancy to injure him
in his occupation."

Weil vs. Israel, 42 La. 955.
Staub vs. Van. Benthuysen, 36 La. 467, etc.

The leading libel case in Louisiana is the case of Miller vs. Holstein, 16 La. 389, in which the principle is declared that "other systems of law may be referred to for light when the great and leading principles of equity are in question and our own laws are silent, but the merely aribtrary rules of a foreign system should not be invoked;" and, that the Article 2315 of the Civil Code governs actions for libel and other damage suits. A long line of decisions has repeatedly upheld this doctrine.

33 An. 957:

"We cannot admit that the Legislative use of
a common law term has introduced in our system
a practice in relation to them."

40 An. 424:

"Our Courts are not bound by the technical
distinctions of the common law."

46 An. 1373:

"Our jurisprudence rejects the common law distinction of words actionable per se requiring no
proof of damage and other words slanderous in
tendency, but exacting proof of damage."

48 An. 914:

> "That the charge preferred against the plaintiff comes clearly within that principle will not be denied—could not be, under the defendant's answer, in view of the fact that under our law and jurisprudence the Courts of this State are not bound by the technical distinction of the common law, etc."

Special attention is called to the case of **Warner vs. Clark & Company, 45 An. 863,** read by counsel in his argument in this case:

> "Under the law of Louisiana libel is a quasi offense, actionable under the broad provisions of the Code 'Every act whatever of man that causes damage to another obliges him by whose fault it happens to repair it.' **Sportono vs. Fourichon, 40 An. 424.**
>
> "Our Courts are not bound by the technical distinctions of the common law as to words actionable per se and not actionable per se. **Miller vs. Holstein, 16 La. 389; Feraz vs. Foote, 12 An. 894; Spotorno vs. Fourichon, 40 An. 424.**
>
> "The extent of damage to credit is an inferential fact arrived at only by an examination of all the circumstances in a case and cannot be the subject of direct proof. Damages or injury may be inferred from the nature of the words written and from the circumstances under which they were written without the necessity of special proof. **Miller vs. Holstein, 16 La. 389; Daley vs. Van Bethuysen, 3 An. 69; Tresca vs. Maddock, 11 An. 206; Cass vs. N. O. Times, 27 An. 214; Spotorno vs. Fourichon, 40 An. 424.**"

Jozsa vs. Moroney, 125 La. 813:

"It is not necessary in matters of libel that the defamation should be made known to the public generally, or even to a considerable number of persons. It is sufficient if it be communicated to only one person other than the person defamed.

"No special damages need be proved. The actual pecuniary damages in an action for libel can rarely be proved and is never the sole rule af assessment. **Mental suffering alone** can be made the basis for damages."

Graham vs. Western Union Tel. Co., 109 La. 1070:

"Suit against a telegraph company for failure to deliver a message to a mother announcing the mortal illness and approaching death of a son. The suit was dismissed in the Court of Appeal upon an exception of 'no cause of action,' for the reason assigned that 'mental pain and anguish resulting from simple actionable negligence is not sufficient basis for an action for damages, if unattended by injury to person, property, health, or reputation.'

"The exception should have been overruled. Under the laws of Louisiana, it is not well grounded. The judgment is reversed, and the cause remanded to the Court of Appeal, to be by it passed on upon the merits."

And the attention of the Court is respectfully called to the paragraph on page 1072, beginning:

"It is useless for us to refer to the decisions of Courts exercising functions where the common law prevails in regard to which we have to be controlled by local law, etc.''

And also to the paragraph in the same decision, on page 1074, beginning:

> "Mental pain and suffering, as to their existence, are certainly as actual, clear and positive as are intellectual enjoyment and gratification, etc."

107 La., at page 699, the Court cites the case of **Miller vs. Holstein,** and again discards the technical rules of the common law and states:

> "This declaration has been repeated a number of times since."

Martin vs. Picayune, 115 La., 979, where a newspaper published of a physician that by his great skill he had cured a young woman afflicted by a very serious disease and the physician sued for libel, held that the petition set up a good cause of action.

In **Lescale vs. Schwartz, 116 La., 293,** Mr. Justice Provosty speaking for the Court, declared that:

> "The rule in this State as to responsibility for injuries is statutory."

And quoting from the Civil Code he held that,

> "Every act whatever of man that causes damage to another obliges him by whose fault it happened to repair it."

In **Dickinson vs. Hathaway, 122 La., 647,** Mr. Chief Justice Breaux, speaking for the Court, said:

> "Any person who publishes a defamatory letter concerning another so as to bring him into contempt, **ridicule or hatred** (black-letters ours), is guilty of libel."

And the same Justice in **Morasca vs. Item Pub. Co., 126 La., 426,** held that:

> "Legal malice is defined as an act growing out of the wicked or mischievious intention of the mind; an act showing a wanton inclination to mischief, an intention to injure or wrong, and a depraved inclination to disregard the rights of others."

II.

Even the **common law** makes the distinction between a libel and a slander. See **Newell on Slander and Libel,** p. 43, on which a libel is defined, and p. 84, on which a slander or oral defamation is defined.

Under the one, libel, no special damages need be proved, whether the words are libelous **per se** or not, and under the other, slander, it is essential if the words are not actionable **per se.**

In the digest of American cases cited in the above work, on page 50 paragraph 34, it has been held libelous to publish of a man **in writing** or **print** "he is a hog"; to call an attorney a "shyster." To call a man a "skunk." The charge a person with being "a drunkard," "a cuck old," " a tory." To designate an editor of a neighboring newspaper "an ill-natured manikin," "a mouse most magnanimous," "a vermin small." And on page 58, digest of English cases, paragraph 1, it is libelous to write and publish of a man that he is an "an infernal villian," "an impostor," "a hyprocite," "a frozen snake." In paragraph 3, ironical phrase may be a libel calling an attorney "an honest lawyer." To impute to a Presbyterian "gross intolerance" in not allowing his hearse to be used at the funeral of his Roman Catholic servant. Page 60, paragraph 10, it is libelous to call a man a "black-leg" or a "black sheep."

Newell, p. 77:

> "Libels which hold a man up to scorn and ridicule, and to feelings of contempt or execration, impair him in the enjoyment of general society, and injure those imperfect rights of friendly intercourse and mutual benevolence which man has with respect to man."

Illustrations, (page 78): To state in writing that a man "has turned into an enormous swine and lives on lame horses" and "will remain a swine the rest of his days" is libelous.

Digest of English cases, on the same page, paragraph 1:

> "Scandalous matter is not necessary to make a libel. It is enough if the defendant induce an ill

opinion to be had of the plaintiff, or to make him **contemptible** or **ridiculous.''**

''To **say** of a man he is a dishonest man is **not** actionable, but to **publish** so or to put in upon posts is actionable. **Skinner 124.''**

III.

ACTS COMPLAINED OF; ACTS OF THE GRAND LODGE.

Townsend on Slander and Libel, Sec. 265:

''If an officer, etc., is guilty of **slander,** he is personally liable. But the publication of a libel by a corporation makes it liable.''

10 Cyc. 1067:

''Corporations are estopped from repudiating the acts of its officers or agents, within **apparent** scope of duties.''

10 Cyc. 1203:

''Corporations responsible for torts, same footing as individuals.''

''Liable for acts of agent even if he exceeded his orders, or; without orders, or,

''1205, against orders.''

If its lawfully constituted agent publish a libel of and concerning any person, while acting unlawfully, but within the apparent scope of his authority, the corporation is liable to respond in damage therefor.

The edicts complained of are therefore the acts of the corporation, directed against the plaintiff, by its duly constituted agent, within the scope of his duties and the corporation is responsible for his official acts. (See **Tr.** 198.)

"Qui facit per alium facit per se."

IV.

CHARITABLE ORGANIZATION.

It is claimed by counsel for defendant, and with apparrent sincerity that being organized under the law of benevolent and charitable institutions, without stock or capital, the defendant is exempt from liability to respond for its torts.

Suffice it to say that exemption from execution of judgment against the corporation is not granted to it by its charter and no such exemption nor any other can be pleaded or exercised except when specially granted by its Sovereign, the State of Louisiana. And this is shown by the fact that it required a special act of the Legislation, Act 225 of 1855, to exempt the corporation from State and Parish taxation of its hall, conditioned with the proviso, ''so long as it (the **hall)** is occupied as the Grand Lodge of the A. Y. Masons.

There is no reason, in law or otherwise, why such a corporation should be exempt from liability for its torts any more than a minister or a priest can shield himself from the consequences of his wrongs, because he has devoted his life to pious or charitable purposes.

V.

DOCTRINE OF CONTRIBUTORY NEGLIGENCE AS APPLIED TO THIS CASE BY DEFENDANT.

Counsel for defendant invokes the doctrine enunciated in the case of **Van Benthuysen vs. Bigney, 36 An. 38**; and offered pamphlet D-2, to show that Bayliss had retaliated in kind:

> "One who is himself at fault cannot recover damages **from another who has retaliated** in kind, although the latter was not justifiable in law, **and** this holds good in spite of the truism that one wrong does not justify another."

This defense has not been pleaded, and parenthetically may be said to be the only defense known to our law which his voluminous answer does not make—and this omission is fatal under our jurisprudence.

Furthermore the case cited above cannot apply to this case. It was a case where an editor of a paper sued another editor of another paper. **Both had been libeling** one another for some time when finally one seemed to have worst of the fray and he sued his adversary. The Court decided the case on the the theory that

> "a man who, himself, commenced a newspaper war, cannot subsequently come to the Court, as a plaintiff, to complain that he has had the worst of the fray."

The case is not parallel.

Odgers on Slander and Libel, 228, 219.

The defendant in the present case could have avoided the mischief by limiting its declarations in the edicts, to a statement that it did not recognize the council of which Mr. Bayliss is the head and calling upon those who had joined it, to recant, without assailing the character of Mr. Bayliss and without hurling the libelous epithets at him personally.

Mr. Bayliss had not libeled anybody, much less the Grand Lodge of Louisiana, before the edicts were issued nor even after for that matter. His statement was directed against Mr. Drew and he alone can complain or could have sued on the publication D-2, if it gave him a cause of action. Counsel for defendant will certainly not contend that the Grand Lodge can have a cause of action against Mr. Bayliss, based on that publication.

> "Evidence to show contributory negligence will be excluded when no such defense has been pleaded."

Bulchner vs. City, 112 La. 599.

"Though the plaintiff may have been guilty of negligence and although that negligence may in fact have contributed to the accident, yet if the defendant could, in the result by the exercise of proper care and diligence have avoided the mischief which happened, the plaintiff's negligence will not excuse him. That the doctrine thus enunciated and affirmed by the English Courts is thoroughly supported in this country, there can be no doubt."

McClanahan vs. **R. R. Co.**, 111 La. 781, 791.

PRIVILEGED COMMUNICATIONS.

Newell, p. 477, Par. 65:

"Where a person, acting under a sense of duty, makes a communication which he reasonably believes to be true, he must be careful not to be led away by his **honest indignation into exaggerated or unwarrantable expressions.** The privilege extends to nothing which is not justified by the occasion."

Again, on p. 509, Par. 108:

"A communication made by a person is privileged which a due regard to his own interest renders necessary . He is entitled to protect himself. In such cases, however, it must appear that he was **compelled** to employ the words complained of. **If he could have done all that his duty or interest demanded without libeling or slandering the plain.**

tiff, the words are not privileged. It is very seldom necessary in self-defense to impute evil motives to others or to charge your adversary with dishonesty or fraud."

On page 394, Par. 4:

"The principle on which privileged communications rest, which of themselves would otherwise be libelous, imports confidence and secrecy between individuals, and is inconsistent with the idea of **communication made by a society** or congregation of persons, or by a private company or **corporate body.**"

Merrill, on Newpaper libel at page 59:

"Defendant must sustain burden of proving that the occasion was privileged.

"It may be compared to one who keeps a dangerous animal, and who is bound to so keep it, that it does no harm—if harm ensues he must answer for it."

VI.

INCONSISTENT PLEADINGS.

The trial Judge dismissed the motion made by plaintiff to compel the defendant to elect as to which defense it relied upon—having pleaded a general denial (Tr., p. 11), justification (Tr., p. 17), and claimed that the circulars were privileged, (Tr., p. 18).

We respectfully submit that the learned Judge erred in refusing the motion, as this Court has repeatedly held that:

> "In an action in damages for slander the only defenses are either a denial, or justification or a confession under mitigating circumstances. There is no such thing in law as a half-way jusification. **An answer which sets forth all these defenses equivocates and is inconsistent.**"
> **Williams vs. McManus, 38 A. 161; 10 A. 231; 28 A. 238; 44 A. 938; 104 La. 505; 106 La. 258; 130 La., Schwing vs. Dunlap, not yet reported.**

Considering the general denial (Tr., p. 11) and our objection (Tr., p. 59 and 61) to all testimony tending to prove justification, we ask that all testimony offered thereunder be disregarded by your Honors.

VII.

JUSTIFICATION.

The defendant has attempted to justify, or at least lessen the libelous meaning of the words used, by showing that they had been applied to other persons under other circumstances. The fact that these words may have been used by others under other circumstances does not necessarily justify the defendant in using them in this case against the plaintiff. He must prove the truth of his charges as applied to this plaintiff and can certainly not do so by offering the **ex parte** conclusion of Lodges from other States and historical statements made by authors who may be prejudiced or without giving the plaintiff an opportunity for cross-examination or rebuttal.

Townsend on Libel and Slander, par. 212 and Note (2nd. Ed.)

"There is no such thing in law as a half way justification."

In the instant case there is not a scintilla of proof that Mr. Bayliss has "peddled" degrees; on the contrary the learned counsel for defendant himself admits that he was misinformed. (Tr., p. 131.)

By Mr. Buck:

"I would like to see that commission."

By Mr. Hubert:

"The point is, that Mr. Bayliss did not confer the degrees."

By Mr. Buck:

"That is the point that is irrelevant, there is nothing here before the Court to show that Mr. Bayliss is responsible for what was done by his deputy; he sent his representative here. **I was under the impression that Mr. Bayliss himself conferred the degrees, but I was misinformed.**"

It is respectfully submitted that defendant's plea of justification fails completely in this respect and with it the plea of privilege.

For the same reason, as held in a recent decision of this Court in **Vordenbaumen Lumber Co., vs. Parkerson,** that the words complained of must be proved strictly as alleged in the petition, so must the defendant pleading justification, prove the truth of the libelous statements made by defendant and proved by the plaintiff.

VIII.

BURDEN OF PROOF ON DEFENDANT.

"Having admitted the charge (Tr., p. ....), and issuance of libelous edicts, the burden of proof that he acted, upon probable cause, in honest belief, based upon reasonable grounds, rests upon defendant."

> Vinos vs. Insurance Co., 33 An. 1265; Staub vs. Van Benthuysen, 36 An. 467; Williams vs. McManus, 38 An. 161; Sibley vs. Lay, 44 An. 936.

The precise charge must be justified.

"There is no better settled point in slander than this; the plea must justify the same words contained in the declaration. It is not enough to justify the sentiment contained in the words."

Ency P. and P. Vol. 13, pp. 80, 81.

IX.

DAMAGES.

See **Civil Code 1934, Par. 3.**

Words & Phrases, Vol. 1, p. 156:

"Actual damages in **an** action of libel are such as the plaintiff suffered, if any, on account of the libel or injury, to the **feelings and** character, or **anguish** of mind by **shame; mortification** and **degradation** caused by the publication. **Grace vs. McArthur, 45 Wis. 518, 521; 76 Wis. 641.**

"The term 'actual damages' as used in an action for libel is broad enou ghto include damages for loss of reputation, **shame,** falsehood, etc., etc. **Hearne vs. De Young, 132 Cal. 357.**"

"Injuries to the feelings, and one's social standing are not susceptible of a precise measurement.

still, in cases of this kind or class, such injuries are recognized as legitimate ground of action."

Dufort vs. Abadie, 23 An. 280; 19 An. 322; 17 An. 64; 38 An. 164, Williams vs. McManus; 109 An. 1070, Graham vs. Western Union Telegraph Co.

Weil vs. Israel, 42 An. 955:

"It is conclusive presumption of law that damages have ensued from the mere publication of such libelous statement, and, therefore, no actual damage need be proved. **Proof of particular or actual damages is only required to enhance a recovery.

"It is true that injuries to one's feelings and social standing are not susceptible of precise adjustment, but such injuries are recognized as a legitimate ground of action for reasonable indemnity."
17 An. 64; 19 An. 322; 23 An. 280.

Mequet vs. Silverman, 52 An. 1369:

"Malice upon the one hand and injury upon the other will be presumed (p. 1373.) Law implies that kind of malice which means and is expressed by a grossly negligent or wanton diregard of the rights of others; and while evidence as to actual malice and as to special damages or specific injury was admissible, it is not essential to recovery." (Long line of authorities.)

McClure vs. Martin, 104 La. 496:

"Damages are necessarily due for libel and slander. The law presumes damages to follow from injurious words spoken or uttered against the plaintiff. (Se authorities, p. 507.)

This Court has granted the following sums as compensation in the following cases of slander and libel:

$5,000.00 for libel. Schwing vs. Dunlap, 130 La.....

$5,000.00 for libel, Luzenberg, vs. O'Malley, 116 La. 699

$1,000.00 for malicious words, 19 An. 322.

$1,000.00 for slanderous epithets, 17 An. 64.

$500.00 for slanderous words, 38 An. 162.

$500.00 for slanderous words, 104 La. 180.

Simpson vs. Robinson, $25.00 held inadequate, increased to $500.00.

$5000.00 for libel. **Schwing vs.**........... **La.**......

X.

Then, it is believed, the mind and unbiased judgment of the Court will be led to consider what substantial amount in dollars and cents would be reasonable compensation to plaintiff, in view of his presumed and proven good standing among men, and in view of his forty years of honorable masonic life among masons; his undisputed blameless life as a citizen. What sum of money ought to partially compensate him for being so publicly defamed, for all agree that it is impossible to measure in money full compensation.

The Court will then consider the standing record, published to the world. There is no telling what harm may result or how his good name may suffer after he is gone.

The Court will, we respectfully submit see that the powerful force of sixteen thousand members of the Craft has been leveled against a single individual—in **concentrated, deliberate aim and expressed purpose to ''crush'' him;** and with absolute disregard for his rights either as a Mason or a man, to bring him into public contempt, ridicule and hatred. He had not wronged one of them. The Court will not forget that the Grand Lodge of Louisiana, voluntarily tendered its services and wonderful strength for the destruction of both the man and his competitive Rite.

''The same reasons that the Supreme Court found in the **Fatjo case, 109 La. 699,** for increasing the damages found by the jury because of the brutal act of slandering one in the family presence, is found here in the fact that the wanton malignment was by the whole masonic family here upon the character of a member of the general family. The thrust was far more stinging to plaintiff and much more effective in its intended injury than if it had been made by a non-masonic body. In direct accusation and sneaking innuendo it could not be made more powerful than when coming from a brotherhood.

Fatjo called Mrs. Seidel a "thief" in the presence of her family only; a jury awarded her $200.00, and this Court affirmed the finding but increased the damages to $500.00. That was an action for slander, and slander is considered in law not one-half as offensive as libel. In the case at bar we have publication equivalent to "thief," read by many thousands and doubtless taken notice of and discussed by as many families. We invoke the proportionate rule, and we respectfully submit that the Court should make the penalty severe enough to forever deter others from defaming the character of citizens under similar circumstances.

Let the punishment fit the crime.

We respectfully ask that the judgment of the lower Court be set aside, and for a judgment in favor of plaintiff and appellant for such sum as this Court, in its discretion, after considering the nature, and circumstances of the case, will deem proper and sufficient.

Respectfully submitted,

L. A. HUBERT,

MONROE McCLURG,
Attorneys for Plaintiff and Appellant.